PLANETS

NEPTUNE

Alexis Roumanis

LET'S READ
AV2 BY WEIGL
ADDED VALUE • AUDIO VISUAL

www.av2books.com

LET'S READ
AV2
BY WEIGL™
ADDED VALUE • AUDIO VISUAL

AV² provides enriched content that supplements and complements this book. Weigl's AV² books strive to create inspired learning and engage young minds in a total learning experience.

Go to **www.av2books.com**, and enter this book's unique code.

BOOK CODE

X439297

AV² by Weigl brings you media enhanced books that support active learning.

Your AV² Media Enhanced books come alive with...

Audio
Listen to sections of the book read aloud.

Video
Watch informative video clips.

Embedded Weblinks
Gain additional information for research.

Try This!
Complete activities and hands-on experiments.

Key Words
Study vocabulary, and complete a matching word activity.

Quizzes
Test your knowledge.

Slide Show
View images and captions, and prepare a presentation.

... and much, much more!

Published by AV² by Weigl
350 5th Avenue, 59th Floor New York, NY 10118
Websites: www.av2books.com   www.weigl.com

Library of Congress Cataloging-in-Publication Data

Roumanis, Alexis, author.
  Neptune / Alexis Roumanis.
     pages cm. -- (Planets)
  Includes index.
  ISBN 978-1-4896-3296-8 (hard cover : alk. paper) -- ISBN 978-1-4896-3297-5 (softcover : alk. paper) -- ISBN 978-1-4896-3298-2 (single user ebook)
-- ISBN 978-1-4896-3299-9 (multi-user ebook)
  1. Neptune (Planet)--Juvenile literature. I. Title.
  QB691.R68 2016
  523.48--dc23
                                    2014041520

Printed in the United States of America in Brainerd, Minnesota
1 2 3 4 5 6 7 8 9 0 19 18 17 16 15

022015
WEP081214

Project Coordinator: Katie Gillespie Art Director: Terry Paulhus

Weigl acknowledges Getty Images and iStock as the primary image suppliers for this title.

What Is Neptune?

Neptune is a planet. It moves in a path around the Sun. Neptune is the eighth planet from the Sun.

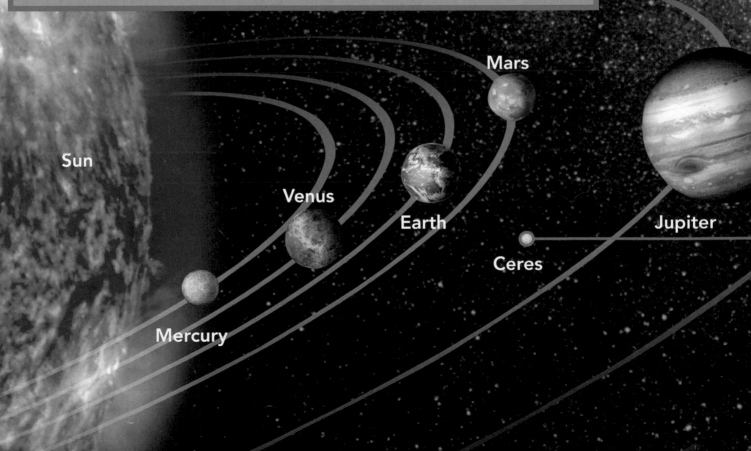

Sun

Mercury

Venus

Earth

Mars

Ceres

Jupiter

NEPTUNE

CONTENTS

3

Eris

Makemake

Haumea

Pluto

Neptune

Uranus

Saturn

Dwarf Planets

Dwarf planets are round objects that move around the Sun. Unlike planets, they share their part of space with other objects.

How Big Is Neptune?

Neptune is the fourth largest planet in the solar system. It is almost four times as wide as Earth.

What Is Neptune Made Of?

Neptune is a large planet made of ice. It is called an ice giant. Neptune also has a rocky center.

Earth

Neptune

7

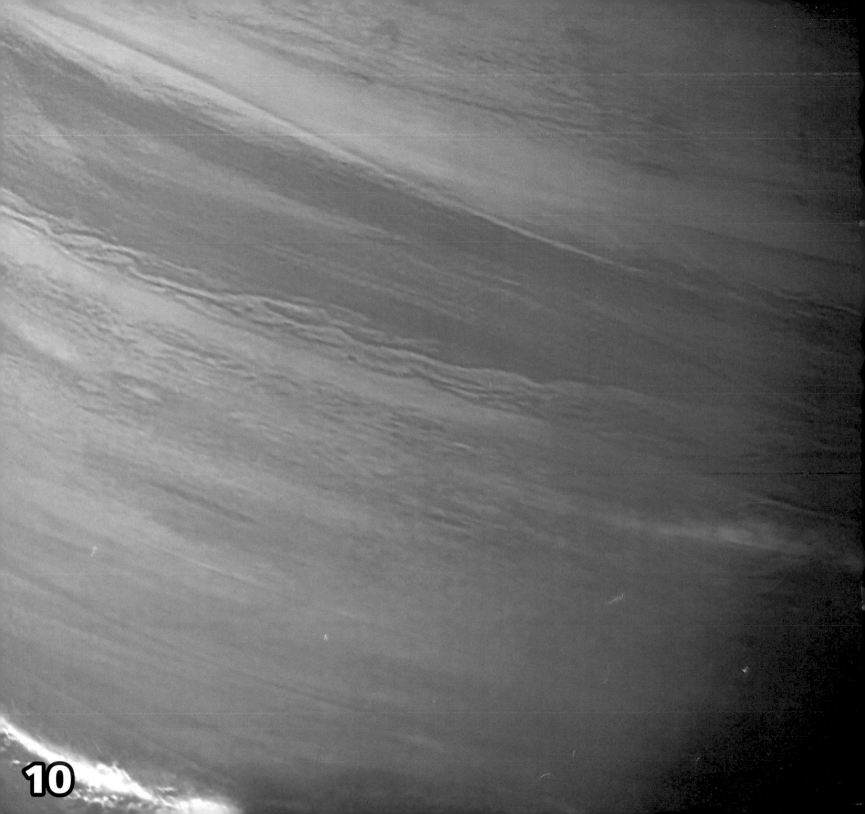

10

9

What Are Dark Spots?

Neptune has many dark spots. They are very strong storms on the planet. Neptune has the fastest winds in the solar system.

What Does Neptune Look Like?

Neptune looks like it has stripes.
These stripes are gas clouds.
Gas clouds make the planet
look blue.

14

What Are Neptune's Moons?

Neptune has 13 known moons. One of these moons has active volcanoes. It is called Triton.

Triton

Who Discovered Neptune?

Urbain Le Verrier helped discover Neptune in 1846. He used math to find the planet.

How Is Neptune Different from Earth?

Each planet is a different temperature.
Neptune is much colder than Earth.
It is one of the coldest planets in the
solar system.

How Do We Learn about Neptune Today?

Telescopes make far away objects look closer. *Hubble* is a special space telescope. It takes pictures of Neptune from space.

NEPTUNE FACTS

This page provides more detail about the interesting facts found in the book. They are intended to be used by adults as a learning support to help young readers round out their knowledge of each planet featured in the *Planets* series.

Pages 4–5

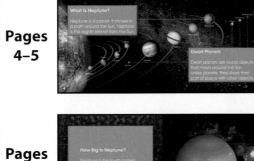

Neptune is a planet. Planets are round objects that move around, or orbit, a star, with enough mass to clear smaller objects from their orbit. Earth's solar system has eight planets, five known dwarf planets, and many other space objects that all orbit the Sun. Neptune is 2,795 million miles (4,498 million kilometers) from the Sun. It takes 60,190 Earth days for Neptune to make one orbit around the Sun.

Pages 6–7

Neptune is the fourth largest planet in the solar system. It is nearly four times the size of Earth. Gravity is a force that pulls objects toward a planet's center. The force of gravity is stronger on Neptune than it is on Earth. A 100-pound (45-kilogram) object on Earth would weigh 114 pounds (52 kg) on Neptune.

Pages 8–9

Neptune is a large planet made of ice. An atmosphere is made of gases that surround a planet. Ice giants have more ice in their atmospheres than other planets. Neptune's atmosphere gradually becomes liquid. The planet's rocky core is about the size of Earth. There is no solid ground on Neptune like there is on Earth. The planet is believed to be mostly made of water, ammonia, and methane.

Pages 10–11

Neptune looks like it has stripes. Like the planet Uranus, methane gas in the atmosphere gives Neptune its color. As sunlight passes through Neptune's atmosphere, methane gas absorbs the red rays of light. An unknown gas absorbs the green rays of light. When the sunlight is reflected back into space by Neptune's cloud tops, it appears blue.

Neptune has many dark spots. Scientists have discovered that the dark spots can last for several years. Eventually, they disappear and new ones take their place. One of these spots, called the Great Dark Spot, was larger than Earth. Winds on Neptune can reach speeds of 1,300 miles (2,092 km) per hour. This is nine times stronger than winds on Earth.

Neptune has 13 known moons. The largest of these is called Triton. It is one of four known bodies in the solar system to have active volcanoes. Triton orbits Neptune in the opposite direction from the other moons. It is one of the coldest places in the solar system. The surface temperature on Triton can fall to -391° Fahrenheit (-235° Celsius).

Urbain Le Verrier helped discover Neptune in 1846. He was a French astronomer who often studied the sky. Le Verrier noticed that something kept pulling Uranus off its orbit. He thought that it must be the mass of another planet. Using math, Le Verrier predicted the location of this mysterious planet. He told another astronomer his idea and Neptune was quickly found.

Each planet is a different temperature. The average temperature on Neptune is -373° F (-225° C). On Earth, the average temperature is 46° F (8° C). Neptune is so much colder than Earth because it is 30 times farther from the Sun. Neptune's south pole is slightly warmer than anywhere else on the planet. Earth's south pole is colder than most places on the planet.

Telescopes make far away objects look closer. Special telescopes, such as the *Hubble Space Telescope*, can take pictures in space. The National Aeronautics and Space Administration (NASA) uses *Hubble* to learn more about Neptune. In 2013, *Hubble* was used to find a new moon orbiting Neptune. This provisional moon is 100 million times less bright than the faintest star in the night sky.

KEY WORDS

Research has shown that as much as 65 percent of all written material published in English is made up of 300 words. These 300 words cannot be taught using pictures or learned by sounding them out. They must be recognized by sight. This book contains 55 common sight words to help young readers improve their reading fluency and comprehension. This book also teaches young readers several important content words. These words are paired with pictures to aid in learning and improve understanding.

Page	Sight Words First Appearance
4	a, around, Earth, from, in, is, it, moves, the, what
5	are, of, other, part, that, their, they, with
6	almost, as, big, four, how, times
8	also, an, has, large, made
11	does, like, look, make, these
12	many, on, very
15	one
16	find, he, to, used, who
19	different, each, much, than
21	about, away, do, far, learn, pictures, takes, we

Page	Content Words First Appearance
4	Neptune, path, planet, Sun
5	dwarf planets, objects, space
6	solar system
8	center, ice, ice giant
11	blue, gas clouds, stripes
12	dark spots, storms, winds
15	moons, Triton, volcanoes
16	math, Urbain Le Verrier
19	temperature
21	*Hubble*, telescopes

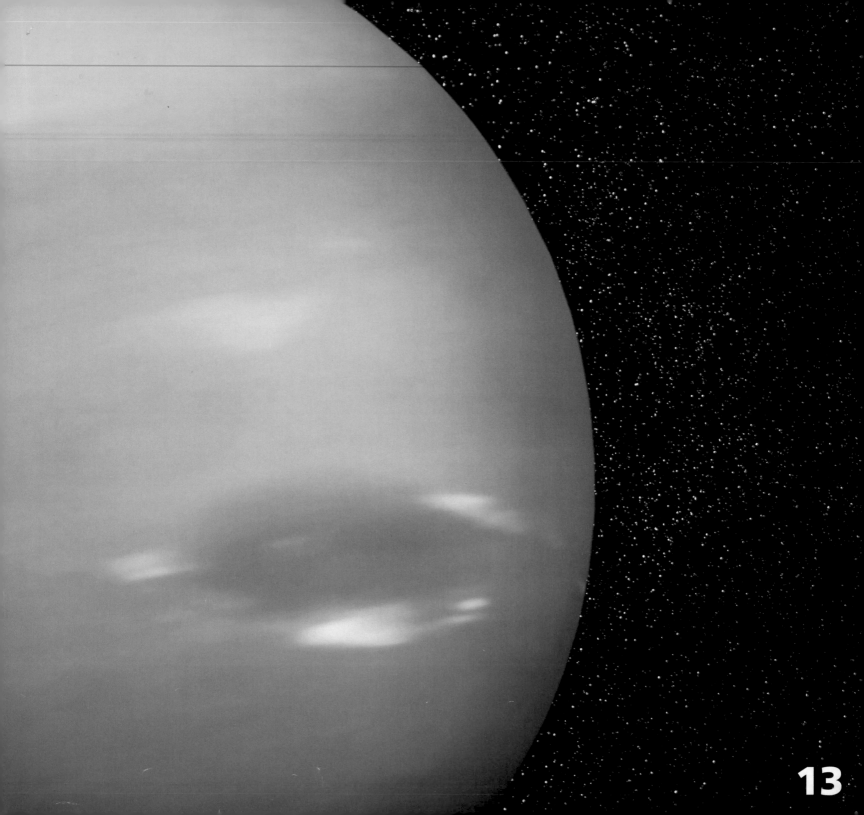

13